D1741494

Digitized by the Internet Archive
in 2013

http://archive.org/details/guidetostpaulsca00leef

QUEEN ANNE.

A GUIDE

TO

ST. PAUL'S CATHEDRAL;

INCLUDING

A COPY OF THE

JNSCRIPTIONS ON THE MONUMENTS,

WITH

Numerous Wood Engravings.

NEW EDITION.

LONDON:

HILL, PRINTER, 48, NORTHAMPTON STREET,
CLERKENWELL.

CONTENTS.

Public Expense of some of the Monuments.

£	Names.	Situation.	Sculptors.
6300	Abercromby, Sir R.	S. Transept ...	*Westmacott.*
	Babington, Dr.	S. W. Trans. ...	*Behnes.*
	Blomfield, Bishop	Ch. S. Aisle ...	*Richmond.*
1575	Bowes, General	N. E. Amb. ...	*Chantrey.*
1575	Brock, Sir Isaac	S. W. Amb. ...	*Westmacott.*
5250	Burges, Captain	S. W. Aisle ...	*Banks.*
1575	Cadogan, Colonel	S. E. Amb. ...	*Chantrey.*
	Cavalry Memorial	Nave...	
	Cockerell, C. R.	N. W. Amb. ...	
4200	Collingwood, Lord.........	S. Transept ...	*Westmacott.*
1575	Cook, Captain..............	Crypt	*Westmacott.*
	Cooper, Sir Astley	S. Transept ...	*Bailey.*
6300	Cornwallis, Marquis	S. Transept ...	*Rossi.*
2100	Crauford, General.........	N. Transept ...	*Bacon, Junr.*
	Crimean Memorial	Nave	*Marochetti.*
	Donne, Dean	Ch. S. Aisle ...	*Stone.*
1575	Duff, Captain	Crypt............	*Bacon, Junr.*
2100	Duncan, Lord	N. Transept ...	*Westmacott.*
3150	Dundas, General.	N. Transept ...	*Bacon, Junr.*
	Elphinstone, M.	N. Aisle.........	*Noble.*
4200	Faulknor, Captain	N. Transept ...	*Rossi.*
	Gibbs, General	S. Transept ...	*Westmacott.*
1575	Gillespie, General	S. Transept ...	*Chantrey.*
2100	Gore, General..............	N. Transept ...	*Chantrey.*
	Hallam, Henry	N. E. Amb. ...	*Theed.*
1575	Hardinge, Captain	S. Transept ...	*Manning.*
1575	Hay, General Sir A.	N. Transept ...	*Hopper.*
2100	Heathfield, Lord	S. Transept ...	*Rossi.*
	Heber, Bishop..............	Ch. S. Aisle ...	*Chantrey.*
1575	Hoghton, General	N. W. Amb. ...	*Chantrey.*
	Hoste, Sir Wm.............	S. Transept ...	*Campbell.*
	Howard, J.	S. Aisle.........	*Bacon.*
6300	Howe, Earl	S. Transept ...	*Flaxman.*
	Johnson, Samuel	N. Aisle	*Bacon.*

£	Names.	Situation.	Sculptors.
	Jones, Sir Wm.	W. Amb.	*Bacon, Junr.*
	Jones, General	S. E. Amb.	. *Behnes.*
	Langworth, General	N. Transept ..	*Manning.*
	Lawrence Sir H.	S. Transept ...	*Lough.*
1575	Le Marchant, General ..	N. E. Amb. ...	*Rossi.*
	Loch, Captain	Nave	
	Lyons, Lord	Nave	*Noble.*
	Lyons, Captain	Nave	
2100	Mackenzie, General	N. Transept ...	*Manning.*
	Mackinnon, General ...	N. Transept ...	*Bacon, Junr.*
	Malcolm, Sir P.	N. W. Amb. ...	*Bailey.*
	Middleton, Bishop	S. W. Aisle ...	*Louth.*
	Miller, Captain	S. Transept ...	*Flaxman.*
	Milman, Dean	Ch. S. Aisle ...	*Williamson.*
4200	Moore, Sir John	S. Transept ...	*Bacon, Junr.*
	Mosse, Captain	N. Transept ...	*Rossi.*
1575	Myers, Sir Wm.	N. W. Amb. ...	*Kendrick.*
	Napier, Chas J.	N. Transept ...	*Adams.*
	Napier, Chas.	N. Aisle	*Adams.*
	Napier, W. F. P.	N. Transept ...	*Adams.*
6300	Nelson, Lord	S. Transept ...	*Flaxman.*
2100	Pakenham, General	S. Transept	*Westmacott.*
3150	Picton, Sir T.	N. Transept ...	*Gahagan.*
3150	Ponsonby, Sir Wm.	N. Transept ...	*Bailey.*
	Reynolds, Sir Joshua ...	Nave	*Flaxman.*
4200	Riou, Captain	N. Transept ...	*Rossi.*
6300	Rodney, Lord	N. Transept ...	*Rossi.*
1575	Ross, General	S. E. Amb.	*Kendrick.*
	Skerrett, General	N. Transept ...	*Chantrey.*
2100	St. Vincent, Earl	N. Transept ...	*Bailey.*
	Torrens, General	W. Amb.	
	Turner, J. W.	S. Transept ...	*Macdowell.*
	Wellington, Duke of ...	Consistory Court	*Stevens.*
4200	Westcott, Captain	S. W Aisle	*Banks.*
	57th Regiment	Nave	*Forsyth.*
	77th Regiment	Nave...............	*Noble.*

THE DUKE OF WELLINGTON'S FUNERAL CAR.

A GUIDE

TO

ST. PAUL'S CATHEDRAL.

THE Cathedral is open daily (Sundays excepted), from 9 a.m., until 5 p.m. Week day services, 8 and 10 a.m., 4 and 8 p.m. Sunday services, 8 and 10.30 a.m., 3.15 and 7 p.m.

Visitors have free access between the services on week days, to view the dome, nave, transepts and monuments; the other parts are shown on payment of the following fees, viz: Crypt, 6d., Library, Clock, and Galleries, 6d., and the Ball, 1s. 6d. for each person.

In order to follow the various objects of interest and importance described in this book, the visitor will observe that it commences at the North door.

Over the door is the Tablet to Sir C. Wren, which formerly stood at the entrance to the choir; the inscription, in latin, is as follows:—

Subtus conditur hujus Ecclesiæ et urbis
Conditor CHRISTOPHOROS WREN, qui vixit
annos ultra nonaginta, non sibi sed bono publico.
Lector, si monumentum requiris, circumspice.
Obiit 25 Feb. ætatis 91; An. 1723.

Translated, it is as follows:

Underneath is buried Sir Christopher Wren,
the builder of this church and city,
Who lived about ninety years,
not to himself, but to the public good.
Reader, if thou seekest his monument, look around.
He died, Feb. 25, 1723, in the 91st year of his age.

We now come to a monument executed by Sir Francis Chantrey, from a design of the late Mr. Tollemache. It represents Fame consoling Britannia for the loss of her heroes; and the following is the inscription on it:

Erected at the public expense, to the memory of
Major-Generals ARTHUR GORE, and
JOHN BYNE SKERRETT,
who fell gloriously, while leading the troops
to the assault of the fortress of Bergen-op-Zoom,
on the night of the 8th and 9th of March, 1814.

The next is Napier's monument, by G. G. Adams, the inscription is as follows:—

CHARLES JAMES NAPIER,
A Prescient General.
A Beneficent Governor.   A Just Man.
Born 1782.   Died 1853.

Next to this is the monument of Sir William Ponsonby, whose horse broke down under him in the battle of Waterloo, and left him to the lances of the French curassiers, before help could reach him. The sculpture, designed by Mr. Theed, and executed by Mr. E. H. Bailey, represents the horse falling exhausted to the earth, whilst his master at the moment of death, is receiving a wreath of laurel from the hands of Victory. The inscription is as follows

Erected at the public expense to the memory of
Major-General the Hon. SIR WILLIAM PONSONBY,
who fell gloriously in the Battle of Waterloo,
on the 18th of June, 1815.

The visitor should now turn round, and observe on the right, against the great pier and almost opposite the entrance, a statue by Mr. Westmacott, of Admiral Lord Duncan, with his boat-cloak or dreadnought round him, his hands grasping his sword, which is laid across him. The pedestal represents, in alto relievo, a sailor, with his wife and child; indicating the veneration felt for this illustrious man by the humblest seamen and their families. The monument is thus inscribed :

Erected at the public expense to the memory of
ADAM, LORD VISCOUNT DUNCAN,
as a testimony of his distinguished eminence
in the naval service of his country;
and as a particular memorial of the
glorious and important victory,
which he gained over the Dutch fleet,
on the 11th of October, 1797
He died on the 4th of August, 1804.

Passing on, in this which is called the north transept, we see in the recess under the east window, a monument by Mr. Charles Rossi, consisting of an insulated base, charged with a sarcophagus, on the front of which Victory and Fame are placing medallions of the deceased officers, commemorated in the following epitaph :

The Services and Death
of two valiant and distinguished Officers,
JAMES ROBERT MOSSE, Captain of the *Monarch*,
and EDWARD RIOU, of the *Amazon*,
who fell in the attack upon Copenhagen, conducted
by Lord Nelson, 2nd of April, 1801, are commemorated
by this Monument, erected at the national expense.

JAMES ROBERT MOSSE, was born in 1746: he served as Lieutenant several years, under Lord Howe, and was promoted to the rank of Post Captain in 1790.

To EDWARD RIOU, who was born in 1762, an extraordinary occasion was presented in the early part of his service, to signalize his intrepidity and presence of mind which were combined with the most anxious solicitude for the lives of those under his command, and a magnanimous disregard of his own.

When his ship, the *Guardian*, struck upon an island of ice, in December, 1789, and afforded no prospect but that of immediate destruction to those on board;

Lieut. Riou encouraged all who desired to take their chance of preserving themselves in the boats, to consult their safety; but judging it contrary to his own duty to desert the vessel, he neither gave himself up to despair, nor relaxed his exertions; whereby, after ten weeks of the most perilous navigation, he succeeded in bringing his disabled ship into port; receiving his high reward of fortitude and peseverance from the Divine Providence, on whose protection he relied.

Adjoining is a panel monument to Admiral Charles Napier, represented as a bust of the gallant Admiral, surrounded by naval emblems, by G. G. Adams; the following is the inscription:

CHARLES NAPIER, M.P,
Admiral,
Count Napier of St. Vincent.
Born 1786.   Died 1860.

Passing on towards the choir, we arrive at Hallam's monument, which is thus inscribed:

HENRY HALLAM,
The Historian of the Middle Ages of the constitution of his country, and of the literature of Europe.

This monument is raised by many friends, who regarding the soundness of his learning, the simple eloquence of his style, his manly and capacious intellect, the fearless honesty of his judgments, and the moral dignity of his life, desire to perpetuate his memory within these sacred walls, as of one who has best illustrated the English Language, the English Character, and the English Name.
Born July 9th, 1777.   Died January 21st, 1859.

W. Theed, Sculp.

On the right, in the ambulatory above, we find a tabular monument by Sir F. Chantrey, in which Major Gen. Bowes is represented in the act of storming the forts of Salamanca. There is the steep breach of a shattered wall, crowded with the enemy, and covered with the slain; the General is leading his troops on to the charge with fixed bayonets, at his feet lies the French standard bearer, who has fallen; -

but in the very moment of victory he himself receives a mortal wound, and sinks into the arms of one of his soldiers. The inscription is brief:

Erected at the public expense to the memory of
Major-General FOORD BOWES,
who fell gloriously, on the 27th June, 1812, while leading
the troops to the assault of the forts of Salamanca.

In the opposite panel, on the left, over the door, is the monument of Major-General Le Marchant, designed by the late James Smith, and executed by Mr. C. Rossi, The genius of Spain is represented placing trophies of victory on the hero's tomb, and bewailing his fall; Britannia, seated, is pointing the attention of a military cadet to the monument, as if to inspire the British youth with emulation of the warrior's fame. Here is the inscription:

Erected at the public expense to the memory of
Major-General JOHN GASPARD LE MARCHANT,
who fell gloriously in the battle of Salamanca,
July the 22nd, 1812.

We now reach the iron gate, leading into the north aisle, and here, against the north-east pier, stands the statue of Dr. Johnson, by Bacon, who is represented with a scroll in his hands, and in the attitude of profound thought. The following inscription on the pedestal was written by Dr. Parr:

A  Ω

SAMUELI JOHNSON,
Grammatico . et . critico
Scriptorum . anglicorum . litterate . perito
Poetæ . luminibus . sententiarum
et . ponderibus . verborum . admirabili
magistro . virtutis . gravissimo

homini . optimo . et . singularis . exempli
qui . vixit . ann . LXXV . Mens . II . dieb . XIII.
deccesit . idib . decembr . ann . Christ . cIɔ . Iɔcc
LXXXIIII . sepult . inæd . sanct . Petr . Westmonasteriens
XIII . kal . Januar . ann . Christ . cIɔ . Iɔcc . LXXXV.
amici . et . sodales . litterarii
pecunia . conlata
H. M. Faciund, Curaver.
On one side of the monument:
Faciebat Johannes Bacon, Sculptor.
Ann. Christ. M.DCC.LXXXXV.

Crossing the entrance to the choir, we find in front of
the massive south-eastern pier, the Marble Pulpit, which
forms a graceful memorial to the memory of a brave Officer,
Captain FITZGERALD, who served in India, and which
his fellow-officers and friends have feelingly contributed
to erect in remembrance of his bravery and virtues.

The Pulpit is entirely constructed of marble of the most
varied and costly description, and apart from its great
æsthetic qualities as designed by Mr. Penrose, architect
to the Cathedral, it displays an example of genuine poly-
chromatic art in combination of the most satisfactory
description; and of its particular class, it may be safely
pronounced amongst the very best specimens of the kind
hitherto produced in England. The total height of this
unique work of modern art is 10 feet $2\frac{1}{2}$ inches from the
floor line, and the diameter at its base is 6 feet $10\frac{1}{4}$ inches.

We now proceed to the South Aisle, at the eastern end
of which, and near the gate leading into choir, we find
one of the most beautiful monuments in the Cathedral,—a
splendid statue (by Sir Francis Chantrey), of Bishop
Heber, kneeling, with one hand upon his breast, and the
other resting upon the Bible. On the pedestal he is represented confirming two Indian converts. Below is the
following inscription:

To the Memory of
REGINALD HEBER, D.D., Lord Bishop of Calcutta,
this Monument was erected by those who loved and
admired him.   His character exhibited a rare union
of fervent zeal with universal tolerance,
of brilliant talent with sober judgment,
and was especially distinguished by Christian humility,
which no applause could disturb, no success abate.
He cheerfully resigned prospects of eminence at home
in order to become
the chief missionary of Christianity in the East;
and having in the short space of three years
visited the greater part of India,
and conciliated the affections and veneration
of men of every class of religion,
he was there summoned to receive the reward of his
labours, in the 43rd year of his age, 1826.

Returning through the South Aisle, in the recess under
the centre window, we find an elegant monument by Geo.
Richmond, representing the recumbent figure of Bishop
Blomfield, many years Bishop of London.   The inscription
in latin, is as follows:

CAROLVS JACOBVS BLOMFIELD, Episc: Ascede
Cestrensi in Londin: Translatvs A. S. MDCCCXXVIII.
Post eximios labores Deo et Ecclesiæ Consecratos in
Christo obdarmivit non: Avg: MDCCCLVII Vixit Ann:
LXXII.

Just near, in a niche in the wall, has been recently
placed, the only perfect monument saved from the old St.
Paul's that of Dr. DONNE, sculptured in his shroud by
Nicholas Stone.   He was Dean of the Cathedral from
1621 to 1631.   The following is the inscription, in latin:
JOHANNES DONNE,
Sac. Theologiæ Professor,
Post variis studiis quibus ab annis tenerrimis
Fideliter nec infeliciter incubuit;
Instinctu et impulsu Sp. Sancti, monitu et hortatu

Regis Jacobi, Ordines Sacros amplexus
Anno sui Jesus 1614, et suæ ætatis 42 ;
Decanatu hujus Ecclesiæ indutus 27 Novembris, 1621,
Exutus morte, ultimo die Martii, 1631 ;
Hic licet in occiduo cineri aspicit Eum
Cujus nomen est oriens.

In the adjoining recess will be found a recumbent figure, by F. J. Williamson, representing the late Dr. Milman, many years Dean of the Cathedral. The monument bears the following latin inscription :

HENRICVS HART MILMAN: Nat. IV. Id. Feb. MDCCXCI. ob. VIII. cal. Oct. MDCCCLXVIII. Pastor-Poeta-Historicvs-Theologvs. Candore Animi : Svavitate Morvm : Capaci Ingenio Insignis. In Omni literarvm genere versatvs veri Indagator. Intrepidvs Sacræ Historiæ Nova scientiarvm Avgmenta Feliciter Adhibvit. Per XIX Annos Hvjvsce Eccles. Cath. Decanvs Navis Solitvdinem Tvrbæ Fidelivm et Divinis Officiis Restitvit. Verbis Christi Sacrosanctis vnice confisvs. Adversos sibi Religioni Secvlvm Si Qvis Alivs Conciliabat. Frvctvs Longi Certaminis Senex Tandem Percepiens.

Leaving the South Aisle, the monument we first approach, is that of John Howard, the philanthropist. It is a well executed statue, by J. Bacon, representing that benevolent man in the Roman costume, trampling on some fetters ; a key in his right hand, and in his left a scroll, on which these words are visible :—"Plan for the Improvement of Prisons and Hospitals." There is a bas-relief on the front of the pedestal, representing Howard entering a cell, bringing food and clothing to the prisoners. Below this is the name " John Howard," on the north side of the pedestal—" John Bacon, Sculptor, 1795," on the south side is the inscription, which was written by

Howard's relation, the late Samuel Whitbread, M.P., and is as follows:

This extraordinary man had the fortune to be honoured,
whilst living, in the manner in which his virtues
deserved. He received the thanks
of both houses of the British and Irish Parliaments
for his eminent services rendered to his country
and to mankind.

Our national prisons and hospitals,
improved upon the suggestion of his wisdom,
bear testimony to the solidity of his judgment,
and to the estimation in which he was held,
in every part of the civilized world,
which he traversed to reduce the sum of human misery,
from the throne to the dungeon, his name was mentioned
with respect, gratitude, and admiration,

His modesty alone
defeated various efforts, which were made during his life,
to erect this statue,
which the public has now consecrated to his memory.
He was born at Hackney, in the county of Middlesex,
September 2nd, 1726.
The early part of his life he spent in retirement,
residing principally upon his paternal estate,
at Cardington, in Bedfordshire,
for which county he served the office of sherriff,
in the year 1773.
He expired at Cherson, in Russian Tartary, on the
20th January, 1790,
a victim to the perilous and benevolent attempt
to ascertain the cause, and find an efficacious remedy
for, the plague.
He trod an open and unfrequented path to immortality,
in the ardent and unremitted exercise of Christian charity.
May this tribute to his fame
excite an emulation of his truly glorious achievements !

———

Over the crypt door is a tabular monument to the memory
of Major General Ross. The sculpture, by Mr. Kendrick,
represents Valour placing an American flag on the departed
hero's tomb, over which Britannia is weeping, while Fame
descends with a laurel wreath to crown his bust.   The
inscription is this :

Erected at the public expense to the memory of
Major General ROBERT ROSS,
Who having undertaken and executed an enterprise
against the city of Washington, the capital of
the United States of America,
which was crowned with complete success,
he was killed shortly afterwards while directing a successful attack upon a superior force, near the city of
Baltimore, on the 12th day of September, 1814.

———

The opposite panel, against the pier, is occupied with a
monument, (by Sir F. Chantrey) of Col. Cadogan, who,
when disabled in battle, desired some of his soldiers to

carry him to an adjoining hill, whence he might witness the issue of the struggle in which he had been engaged. He is depicted in the sculpture borne along by his men, with his face still towards the enemy; one of the French standards (the eagle) with its bearer, lies trodden under foot, and another is flying, while the soldiers who support the wounded officer, seeing the French routed, are waving their hats in triumph. The inscription is brief:

Erected at the public expense to the memory of
Colonel the Hon. HENRY CADOGAN, who fell gloriously
in the command of a Brigade, in the memorable
Battle of Vittoria, 21st of June, 1813,
when a complete victory was gained over the French army
by the allied forces under the Marquis of Wellington:
Colonel Cadogan was son of Charles Sloane, Earl Cadogan,
born 28th of February, 1780.

Near the door is a statue by Behnes. On the pedestal is the following inscription:

Statue of the late
Major General Sir JOHN THOMAS JONES, Bart., K,C.B.,
Erected
by his surviving Brother Officers of the Royal Engineers,
in testimony
of their sense of his high professional attainments,
and of his important military services.
His honourable career
extended from
A.D. 1797 to A.D. 1843.

The visitor should now turn round and inspect Sir H. Lawrence's Monument, nearly opposite the door leading to the Crypt. The following is the inscription:

Sir HENRY MONTGOMERY LAWRENCE, K.C.B.
Born 28th of June, 1806,
Died in the defence of Lucknow, July the 4th, 1857.

On the front of the pedestal is represented the Hero giving encouragement to the imprisoned sufferers, a true model of a christian spirit.　　　　· J. C. Lough, Sculp.

———

Under the East Window, on the left, in the South Transept, is Flaxman's noble monument to Earl Howe. The
statue of this gallant officer represents him with a telescope in his hand, the British lion reposing by his side,
and Britannia, holding her trident, is seated on a pedestal,
upon which History is recording the Earl's exploits, while
Victory, bending forward, places a palm branch in the lap
of Britannia. At the feet of the Admiral is the inscription.

Erected at the public expense to the memory of
Admiral EARL HOWE,
in testimony of the general sense of his great and
meritorious services,
in the course of a long and distinguished life, and in
particular for the benefit
derived to his country, by the brilliant victory which he
obtained over the French fleet, off Ushant, 1st June, 1794.
He was born 19th March, 1726, and died 5th August,
1799, in his 74th year.

———

Adjoining is Westmacott's monument of Admiral Lord
Collingwood. It represents the approach to the shores of
this country of a man-of-war, bringing home the remains
of the gallant officer. The body is stretched upon the
deck, shrouded in colours won from the enemy; and,
while Fame bends over it, Father Thames, (attended by
the genii of other streams) eagerly catching the proclama-
tion of the hero's achievements. There is an alto-relievo
on the gunwale of the vessel, symbolising the progress
of navigation in three stages; man is depicted, first ven-
turing on the ocean, beyond sight of his landmarks, with
the stars for his guide; next with the magnet, ever at his
hand to steer by; and, lastly, forging instruments of war,
to make even the unsteady sea a battle field. The inscription is as follows:

Erected at the public expense to the memory of
CUTHBERT LORD COLLINGWOOD,
Who died in the command of the fleet in the Mediterranean,
on board of the *Ville-de-Paris*,
vii March, MDCCCX, in lxi year of his age.
Wherever he served he was distinguished
for conduct, skill, and courage; particularly in the
action with the French fleet, June 1st, MDCCXCIV,
as Captain of the *Barfleur*;
in the action with the Spanish fleet, xiv February,
MDCCXCVII, as captain of the *Excellent*;
but most conspicuously in the decisive victory off
Cape Trafalgar, obtained over
the combined fleets of France and Spain,
to which he eminently contributed, as vice-Admiral of
the Blue, commanding the larboard division,
xxi October, MDCCCV.

The next is a monument to the memory of Turner, the
celebrated Painter, bearing the following inscription:
JOSEPH WILLIAM MALLORD TURNER, R.A.
Died 19th December, 1851.
P. Macdowell, Sculp.

Against the opposite pier is the statue of Lord Heathfield, by Rossi. This noble officer is in full uniform, and
in the robes of a Knight of the Bath. The pedestal represents the warrior and the British lion, reposing
securely at Gibraltar, while Victory descends to crown
the soldiers with laurel. The inscription is—
Erected at the public expense to the memory of
General GEO. AUG. ELLIOT, LORD HEATHFIELD, K.B.
in testimony of the important services which he rendered
to his country by his brave and gallant defence of
Gibraltar, of which he was Governor,
against the combined attack of the French and Spanish
forces, on the 13th September, 1782.
He died on the 6th July, 1790.

In the South Transept, against one of the great piers,

the visitor will see the monument to the Marquis Corn-wallis, by Mr. C. Rossi. It consists of a group in pyra-midical form, the apex being the statue of the Marquis on a round pedestal; he is robed as a knight of the garter. At the base are several figures, personifying the British empire in Europe and India. The figure of Britannia is not considered happily executed, but the rest are good, as also is the statue of the Marquis. The third figure on the left is intended to signify the Baggareth, one of the rivers of India; the small one on the right, seated on a fish and a calabash, is the Gunga, or as we term it, the Ganges. The inscription runs thus:

To the memory of
CHARLES, MARQUIS CORNWALLIS.

Governor-General of Bengal,
who died 5th of October, 1805, aged 66,
at Ghazepore, in the province of Benares, in his
progress to assume the command of the army in the field.
This monument is erected at the public expense,
in testimony of his high and distinguished public character,
his long and eminent public services, both as a soldier and
a statesman, and the unwearied zeal with which his
exertions were employed in the last moments of his life
to promote the interests and honour of his country.

The panel above contains a tabular monument in honour
of Capt. Miller. It is the work of Flaxman. The figure
head of the Theseus is seen, in which the Captain died,
off the coast of Acre; Britannia and Victory elevate the
hero's medallion against a palm tree, on which are the
words "St. Vincent—Nile." Round the medallion is
inscribed—

To Captain R. WILLET MILLER,
This monument is raised by his companions in victory.

Opposite to Lord Cornwallis's monument is that of
Nelson, by Flaxman; it is placed against one of the great
piers in the South Transept. The admiral is depicted,
arrayed in the robe presented to him by the Sultan; he
leans on an anchor, and a rope is coiled at his feet. On
one side of the pedestal is the British lion; on the other,
Britannia is pointing two young sailors to the hero for
their imitation. On the pedestal itself there are allegorical
representations of the North Sea, the German Ocean, the
Nile, and the Mediterranean. On the cornice, are the
words—" Copenhagen—Nile—Trafalgar." Subjoined is
the inscription on the base:

Erected at the public expense to the memory of
Vice-Admiral HORATIO VISCOUNT NELSON, K.B.
to record his splendid and unparalleled achievements

during a life spent in the service of his country,
and terminated at the moment of victory, by a glorious
death, in the memorable action off Cape Trafalgar,
on the 21st of October, 1805,

Lord Nelson was born on the 29th of September, 1758.
The Battle of the Nile was fought on the 1st of Aug. 1798.
The Battle of Copenhagen on the 2nd of April, 1801.

NELSON.

The panel above contains a tabular monument to Capt.
Hardinge, by the late Mr. C. Manning. An [Indian
warrior, our ally, holds the British standard, and
Fame is placing a wreath upon the hero's name. Beneath
we read—

NATIONAL.

To GEO. N. HARDINGE, Esq.,
Captain of the Fiorenza, 36 guns, 186 men, who attacked

on three successive days, La Piedmontaise, 50 guns, 566 men, and fell near Ceylon, in the path to victory, 8th March, 1808, aged 28 years.

We now turn towards the south door, and, on the east side are Generals Pakenham and Gibbs, sculptured in full uniform, by Westmacott. The inscription is—

Erected at the public expense to the memory of
Major General the Hon. Sir EDWARD PAKENHAM, K.B.
and of Major General SAMUEL GIBBS,
who fell gloriously on the 8th of January, 1815,
while leading the troops to an attack
of the enemy's works in front of New Orleans.

On the other side of the door is Sir F. Chantrey's statue of General Gillespie, with this inscription—

Erected at the public expense to the memory of
Major General ROBERT ROLLO GILLESPIE,
who fell gloriously on the 31st of October, 1814,
while leading the troops to an assault
on the fortress of Kalunga, in the kingdom of Nepaul.

Near to this stands the monument of that eminent and amiable Surgeon, Sir Astley Cooper, sculptured by Bailey.

Sir ASTLEY COOPER, Bart.,
K.C.H., F.R.S.. D.C.L.,
Member of the National Institute of France.
Sergeant Surgeon to their late Majesties
George IV. William IV.
and to her present Majesty Queen Victoria,
and for a period of 42 years
Surgeon to Guy's Hospital.
Born 1768. Died 1842.

Animated by a fervent attachment
to the science and practice of his profession,
It was the study of his life to augment and exemplify
the resources of Surgery,
and by a most assiduous, benevolent and successful
application of his time and talents

to this noble department of the healing art,
not his country alone, but the world,
became indebted to his exertions
and familiar with his Fame;
as a memorial of his excellence and their admiration,
his contemporaries and pupils
have erected this Monument to perpetuate
his name and his example.

———

Opposite, against the great pier, is a statue of Sir Wm. Hoste, by Mr. T. Campbell. It represents this gallant officer in full naval uniform, wearing the cloak of one of his orders of knighthood, leaning against the capstan of his vessel, and with a truncheon in his hand. Beneath his arms is a brief inscription—

Cattaro Lissa
Sir WILLIAM HOSTE, Bart., K.C.B., K.M.T.,
Captain in the Royal Navy,
Erected by his brother Officers
and the admirers of his services.

———

Immediately facing this is the noble monument of Sir John Moore, by Mr. Bacon, Junr., whose burial at midnight on the ramparts of Corunna, is so touchingly described in Charles Wolfe's ode—

"Not a drum was heard, not a funeral note,
As his corpse to the ramparts we hurried."

On the monument, Valour and Victory are lowering him in his grave, by entwined laurel, and the genius of Spain (recognized by the shield with the Spanish arms) plants her standard over his tomb. Beneath is inscribed—

Sacred to the memory of
Lieutenant-General Sir JOHN MOORE, K.B.,
who was born at Glasgow, 1761.
He fought for his country
in America, in Corsica, in the West Indies,
in Holland, Egypt, and Spain;
and on the 16th of January, 1809,
was slain by a cannon ball, at Corunna.

Next under the window, is an equestrian statue of Sir Ralph Abercromby, very ably executed by Westmacott. The horse is careering over the fallen enemy, but the rider sinks, bleeding and faint, into the arms of a Highlander.

LIEU. GEN. SIR RALPH
ABERCROMBY. KB

On the ground, a dying French soldier is vainly endeavouring to reach and recover his lost standard. A sphynx on each side of the monument (the emblem of Egypt) indicates the scene of the hero's exploits. On the pedestal we read—

Erected at 'the public expense to the memory of
' Lieutenant-General Sir RALPH ABERCROMBY, K.B. ·
Commander-in-Chief of an expedition directed against the
French in Egypt; who, having surmounted with consum-
mate ability and valour, the obstacles opposed to his
landing, by local difficulties, and a powerful and well prepared enemy, and having successfully established and
maintained the successive positions necessary for conduct-
ing his further operations, resisted with signal advantage,
a desperate attack of chosen and veteran troops on 21st
March, 1801, when he received in the engagement a
mortal wound, but remained in the field, guiding by his
direction, and animating by his presence, the brave troops
under his command, until they had achieved the
brilliant and important victory obtained on that memorable
day. The former actions of a life spent in the service
of his country, and thus gloriously terminated,
were distinguished by the same military skill,
and by the same zeal for the public service, particularly
during the campaigns of the Netherlands, in 1793 & '94;
in the West Indies in 1796 & '97; and in Holland in 1799;
in the last of which, the distinguished gallantry and
ability with which he effected his landing on the Dutch
Coast, established his positions in the face of a powerful
enemy, and secured the command of the principal fort
and arsenal of the Dutch Republic, were acknowledged
and honoured by the thanks of both Houses of Parliament,
Sir Ralph Abercromby expired on board the *Foudroyant,*
the 28th of March, 1801, in his 66th year.

A few paces will bring us to the monument of Lord
Lyons, by M. Noble, briefly inscribed:

EDMUND LORD LYONS, Admiral, G.C.B. ·
Born 1790.   Died 1858.
Erected by his Friends and Admirers.

· Opposite to this, against the great pier, is a statue of
Dr. Babington, (by Behnes,) in his professional robes,
with the inscription—

WILLIAM BABINGTON, M.D., F.R.S.,
Fellow of the Royal College of Physicians.

born May 21st, 1756, died April 29th, 1833.
Eminently distinguished for science;
beloved for the simplicity of his manners,
and the benevolence of his heart;
respected for his inflexible integrity, and his pure
and unaffected piety.
In all relations of his professional life,
he was sagacious, candid, diligent and humane,
firm in purpose, gentle in execution;
justly confident in his own judgment,
yet generally open to the opinion of others;
liberal and indulgent to his brethren,
but ever mindful of his duty to the public.
To record the admiration of so rare a union of intellectual
excellence and moral worth, and to extend to future
generations the salutary influence which his living
example can no longer diffuse,
this monument has been erected by the public
subscriptions of his contemporaries.
A:D. 1837.

Advancing a few paces, we see above, against the same
pier, a tabular monument to Sir Isaac Brock, by Westmacott, the sword and helmet of the deceased being placed
above it. He is expiring in the arms of a British soldier,
while an Indian is gazing sorrowfully on the scene. The
inscription runs thus—

Erected at the public expense
to the memory of Major-General Sir ISAAC BROCK,
who gloriously fell on the 13th of October,
M.DCCCXII.
in resisting an attack on Queenstown,
in Upper Canada.

In the left hand corner of this, the western ambulatory,
stands Bacon's noble statue of Sir William Jones. This
accomplished philosopher, historian, poet and scholar, is
represented in a studious attitude, his arm resting on the
Institutes of Menu. Against the pedestal, Study and
Genius are unveiling oriental science. The inscription is:

To the memory of
Sir WILLIAM JONES, Knight,
one of the judges of the Supreme Court of Judicature,
at Fort William, in Bengal.
This statue was erected by the Hon. East India Company,
in testimony of their grateful sense of his public services,
their admiration of his genius and learning,
and. their respect of his character and virtues.
He died in Bengal, on the 24th of April, 1794, aged 47.

We have now reached the door of the stairs leading to
the Whispering Gallery; we will pass it however, and
complete our tour on the floor.   Proceeding along the nave
we find in the left panel of the first 'recess, a tabular
monument to Captain Loch.   The Captain, assisted by
his men, is in the act of assaulting the stockades of the
Burmese.   The inscription is as·follows :—

Sacred to the Memory of
GRANVILLE GOWER LOCH.
Companion of the Order of the Bath, Captain of H.M. Ship
Winchester, who fell in the service of his country,
near Donabeu, on the River Irrawaddy,
on the 4th of February, 1853, in the 40th year of his age.

Adjoining, under the window, the visitor will see the
noble monument to Capt. Westcott, by Banks.   The hero
is falling into the arms of Victory, in the battle of the
Nile.   In the bas-relief is seen the explosion of the
French ship *L' Orient*; the Egyptian shore is indicated
by sphynxes and palm trees; the figure recumbent on the
pedestal is taken from an ancient statue of the river Nile.
The inscription runs—

Erected at the public expense, to the memory of
GEORGE BLAGDON WESTCOTT, Captain of the Majestic;
who, after 33. years service, fell gloriously
in the victory obtained over the
French fleet, off Aboukir,

the first day of August, in the year 1798, in the forty-sixth year of his age.

In the right panel is a tabular monument to Captain Lyons, thus inscribed—

Sacred to the Memory of

Captain EDMUND MOWBRAY LYONS, Royal Navy, Son of Rear Admiral Sir Edmund Lyons, Bart. G.C.B., K.C.H.,

Commander-in-chief of Her Majesty's Fleet, in the Black Sea and Mediterranean, under whose orders he engaged the Batteries of Sevastopol, in H.M.S. Miranda, on the 18th of June, 1855, and there was mortally wounded, having just returned from the command of the Squadron in the sea of Azov, where his brilliant successes were warmly acknowledged by his Sovereign;

"Who mourned his loss as one who was so bright an Ornament to the Navy."

Cut off in the prime of Life, the path to the highest earthly honours opening before him.

He died as a Hero and Christian should die.

This tablet is erected in deepest grief by the officers and ship's company of H.M.S. Miranda, who had served under him in the Baltic, White Sea, Black Sea, and the Sea of Azov, and who loved and revered him, possessing as he did, every manly attribute, every endearing quality.

He died on the 23rd of June, 1855. Aged 36.

Proceeding towards the west door, we find in the second recess, the monument of Bishop Middleton, by Louth. His lordship is confirming two Hindoos. The inscription is as follows—

THOS. FANSHAW MIDDLETON, D.D., First Protestant Bishop in India, Consecrated to the See of Calcutta, May 8th, 1814, died July 8th, 1822.

This monument was erected by the joint contribution of Members of the Society for Promoting Christian Knowledge, And the Society for the Propagation of the Gospel.

In the third recess is a Monument to Capt. Burges, finely
executed by Banks. The brave commander is receiving a
sword from the hand of Victory. On the pedestal are
various symbolical representations, in which Defeat and
Captivity are prominent. The inscription is:

Sacred to the memory of
RICHARD RUNDLE BURGES, Esquire,
Commander of His Majesty's Ship *Ardent*,
who fell in the 43rd year of his age,
while bravely supporting the honour
of the British flag.
in a daring and successful attempt to break the enemy's
line, near Camperdown,
on the 11th of October, 1797,
His skill, coolness and intrepidity
eminently contributed to a victory
equally advantageous and glorious to his country.
That grateful country
by the unanimous act of the Legislature,
enrols his name high in the list of those heroes,
who under the blessing of Providence,
have established and maintained her naval superiority,
and her exalted rank among nations.

We now come to the Ecclesiastical or Consistory Court
of the diocese, and used also for the Bishops' triennial
visitation; in which is now erected an elaborate monument
to the great Duke of Wellington, by Stevens. The general
design is architectural, the sarcophagus on which the
effigy rests being of white marble, like the rest of the
work, with rich ornament of bronze formed of military
trophies and floriated wreaths, massive, and rather in the
taste of the Roman decacence as to style. It bears on
each side the simple inscription, "Arthur, first Duke of
Wellington." Above the effigy is an arched canopy, ob-
long in plan, supported on eight white marble columns, the
shafts of which are entirely carved with foliated diaper,

the capitals also foliated in the style of the Italian Renais-
sance, and the frieze of bronze running all round, bearing
cherub heads as the prominent feature in the ornament.
The ceiling of the canopy is also of bronze, formed in
foliated panels with cherub heads in each. On each front
above the centre of the canopy arch is a circular bronze
shield bearing the coat of arms of the Duke, enclosed by
the garter of the Order of the Garter, separate. The
bronze groups fill the space at the two ends upon the cornice of the canopy. They are extremely bold and powerful in the action of the figures, and, projecting above the
entablature, have a very fine effect. Each group is of two
figures. In one a seated female figure represents Truth
plucking out the tongue of Falsehood; in the other a female
figure, also seated, as Valour, holding a club and shield,
thrusts down at her feet a crouching man, as Cowardice.
These figures, which are about life-size, are conceived
with fine artistic feeling, much in the style of Michael
Angelo, without borrowing from the great master, and they
form a most striking and original feature in the design.
It will be understood that this is a monument, and not a
tomb, for Wellington rests in the crypt near to his famous
brother-in-arms, Nelson, whose monument is the well-
known work of Flaxman, in the south transept.

The two end walls of the chapel bear each three fine
bas-reliefs in white marble, the centre one being the largest
and most important in subjects: these are the work of
two sculptors of eminence, Mr. Calder Marshall, R.A., and
Mr. Woodington, A.R.A.

The principal work of Mr. Marshall is a composition of
many figures, in which the women with their children are
especially graceful, suggested, by passages in the Psalms—
" Righteousness and Peace have kissed each other;"
" Young men and maidens, old men and children, praise

the name of the Lord." The smaller reliefs at each side
represent in one Job addressing his friends—"Unto me
men gave ear, and waited, and kept silence at my counsel;"
in another the centurion and our Lord—"I am a man
under authority, having soldiers under me." These are
on the eastern wall; Mr. Woodington's occupy the western
end. The subject of the large relievo is Melchisedec blessing Abraham, a composition containing numerous figures
of men with agricultural implements and weapons, form-
ing the company of the Patriarch, crying, "Blessed be the
Most High God." On one side of this large work is David
praising God with the words, "O, God the Lord, the
strength of my salvation, thou hast covered my head in the
day of battle;" and on the other, John the Baptist holding
the cross, is admonishing the soldiers. These bas-reliefs,
therefore, beyond their excellent merits as works of art,
have a significant and appropriate meaning on the walls
of the chapel dedicated to the memory of a great soldier,
ennobled by his deeds and honoured by his country.

At the end of the nave is the Crimean Monument to the
Officers of the Coldstream Guards. The entablature is
supported by the effigies of two soldiers of the regiment,
bending over a representation of the Tomb on Cathcart's
Hill, in the Crimea, and below it is inscribed their several
names and designations. Baron Marochetti, Sculp.

Sacred to the Memory of
Lieutenant Colonel the Hon. T. VESEY DAWSON,
Lieutenant Colonel J. C. MURRAY COWELL,
Captain LIONEL D. MACKINNON,
Captain the Hon. GRANVILLE C. C. ELLIOTT,
Captain HENRY M. BOUVERIE,
Captain FREDERICK H. RAMSDEN,
Lieutenant EDWARD A. DISBROWE,
Lieutenant C. HERBERT GREVILLE,
of the Coldstream Guards.
Who fell at the Battle of Inkerman, Nov. 5th, 1854.

Brothers in Arms, in Glory, and in Death,
they were buried in one grave.

The whole is surmounted by the colours of the regiment; between which, above the monument, is a tablet bearing the following inscription:

These Colours
Belonged to the Coldstream Regiment of Foot Guards,
And were presented by Col. the Hon. GEO. UPTON, C.B.
and the Officers of the Regiment,
With the sanction of Field Marshal the
EARL OF STRAFFORD, G.C.B. Colonel of the Regiment,
as a tribute
to the gallant and devoted conduct of their comrades
who fell at the Battle of Inkerman,
and whose names are recorded on this Cenotaph.

Crossing the Nave, we come to the Morning Chapel, where there is divine service every morning at eight o'clock. This chapel has been recently decorated in a very elegant manner, the marble work was executed by Messrs. Field, Poole & Co., of Westminster. The Altar is approached by three broad steps, of which the lower ones are encrinital 'birds eye' marble, and the upper step of white Spanish dolomite. At either end is a square return on the same level, terminating with circular pedestals bearing bronze gas standards. This platform is ingeniously inlaid with marbles of the richest and most varied hues. On the upper dais, (which is a high step), is placed the Altar table; and the two ends of the semi-circular apse are filled with curvillinear steps of less height, on the southern side of which, rests a handsome white marble Credence. The whole design, with the elaborate form of the marble pavement, has a very pleasing effect.

The Mosaic in the centre panel at the West end of the Chapel, by Salviati, is in memory of the late Archdeacon Hale, subject "The Risen Saviour," and the stained glass window, is in memory of the late Dean Mansel, subject "The Incredulity of St. Thomas."

Passing up the North-west Aisle, we come to a panel monument to the 57th Regiment, and adjoining, we find the Cavalry Memorial, erected:—

In Memory of the
Officers, Non-Commissioned Officers and Privates
of the Cavalry division of the British Army,
Who fell in action, or died of wounds or disease, during the war with Russia, in the years 1854—1855—1856.

Next to the Cavalry memorial is a panel monument by M. Noble, to the Officers and Men of the 77th Regiment:

To commemorate the loss of
15 Officers, 542 Non-Commissioned Officers, Drummers, and Privates, sustained by the 77th Regiment, during the Crimean campaign, 1854—1856.

On the banner is inscribed:—

77th (East Middlesex) Regiment.
Seringapatam,—Ciudad Rodrigo,—Badajos Peninsula,
Alma,—Inkerman,—Sevastopol.

On each side will be found inscribed the names of the Officers:—

Colonel T. C. EGERTON.	Capt. W. C. DILKE.
Capt. J. NICHOLSON.	Capt. W. B. C. A. PARKER.
Capt. C. E. KNIGHT.	Lieut. F. ALDER.
Lieut. B. H. BROWN.	Surgeon C. MACARTNEY.
Capt. E. H. L. CROFTON.	Capt. W. H. C. G. PECHELL.
Bt. Major B. D. GILBY.	Capt. A. LEMPRIERE.
Lieut. A. WALMESLEY.	Lieut. A. F. MAINE.
Ensign C. H. MASSEY.	

A little further on is a tabular monument:—
To the Memory of
Major-General Sir ARTHUR WELLESLEY TORRENS, K.C.B.
Mortally wounded at the Battle of Inkerman.
Died August 24th, 1855. Aged 46.

Near the above is an imposing Memorial to Lords Melbourne:—
"Through the gate of death, we pass to our joyful resurrection."

WILLIAM VISCOUNT MELBOURNE.	FREDERICK VISCOUNT MELBOURNE.
Prime Minister in the last four years of the reign of King William the IV. And the first four years of the reign of Queen Victoria. Born 1779. Died 1848.	Envoy Plenipotentiary at the Court of Madrid, and Ambassador at the Court of Vienna. Born 1782. Died 1853.
"Until the day break and the Shadows flee away." *Solomon's Song.*	"They that dwell under his shadows shall return." *Hosea* XIV.

In the same recess will be seen two brass tablets, in memory of the Officers, Seamen, Marines and Boys, who lost their lives on September 7th, 1870, when H.M. Ship "Captain," foundered off Cape Finisterre.

Passing on towards the north door, leaving the Lord Mayor's vestry on the left, we come to the statue of Sir Joshua Reynolds, (by Flaxman), in his robes of office as doctor of laws, holding his lectures in his right hand, his left resting on a pedestal, exhibiting a head of Michael Angelo. The inscription is as follows

JOSHUÆ REYNOLDS,
Pictorum sui seculi facile Principi
et splendore, et commissuris colorum
alternis vicibus luminis et umbræ sese mutuo excitantium,
vix ulli-veterum secundo;
qui cum summa artis gloria uteretur; et morum
suavitate et vitiæ elegantia perinde commendaretur
artem etiam ipsam per orbam terrarum
languentem et prope intermortuam,
exemplis egregie venustis suscitavit:
præceptis exquisite conscriptis illustravit
atque emendatiorem et expolitiorem
posteris excercendam tradidit:
Laudem ejus fautores et amici
hanc statuam posuerunt A.S. 1813.
Natus die 16 mensis Julii 1723.
Mortem obiit die 23 Februarii, 1792.

the following is a translation:

To JOSHUA REYNOLDS,
Prince of the Painters of his age,
and in the splendour and harmony of his colouring
bringing forth in turn the varieties of light and shade,
scarcely second to any of the ancient masters:

JOSHUA REYNOLDS

who while invested with the highest glories of his art
became yet more honourable by suavity of manners,
and urbanity of life;
who found his art languishing and decaying over the earth,
and revived it by the force of his admirable example,
illustrated it by rules exquisitely framed, and
delivered it to the hands of posterity corrected and polished.
The friends and guardians of his fame,
placed this statue, in the year of salvation, 1813.
He was born July 16, 1723;
Died, February 23, 1792.

In a panel, near, is a tablet to the late C. R. Cockerell, Surveyor to this Cathedral; and to Ann Maria, his wife.

In the western ambulatory of the north transept, is Major-General Hoghton's monument, by Chantrey. This gallant officer received a mortal wound in the very moment of victory, and expired on the field. He is represented raising himself on the ground, and with his last breath directing his men in their charge. In the back-ground Victory waves the British flag, while extending a wreath of laurel to crown the fallen soldier. The epitaph is simply:

Erected at the public expense
to the memory of
Major-General DANIEL HOGHTON,
who fell gloriously, 16th May, 1811, at Albuera.

The opposite panel commemorates another of the heroes of Albuera. Wisdom and Valour (Minerva and Hercules) unite in pointing to the gallant soldier's bust. The monument is by Mr. Kendrick. The inscription is as follows:

Erected at the public expense to the memory of
Lieutenant-Colonel Sir WM. MYERS, Bart.,
who gloriously fell in the battle of Albuera,
May 16th, 1811, aged 27 years.

His Illustrious commander, the Duke of Wellington, bore this honourable testimony to his services and abilities, in a letter to Lady Myers, written from Elvas, May 20, 1811.

"It will be some satisfaction to you to know that your son fell in an action, in which, if possible, the British troops surpassed all their former deeds, and, at the head of the Fusilier Brigade, to which a great part of the final success of the day was to be attributed. As an officer he had already been highly distinguished, and, if Providence had prolonged his life, he promised to become one of the brightest ornaments to his profession, and an honour to his country."

Next to this stands the monument of Sir Pulteney Malcolm, by Bailey, rather larger than life. Sir Pulteney, who has his naval cloak thrown over his shoulders, and a telescope under his arm, was Captain of the *Donegal*, under Lord Nelson. A gale of wind made it impossible for him to reach Trafalgar until the victory was won, but he was able then to do great service in rescuing numbers of brave seamen from the waves, as the confusion was subsiding. On the pedestal is the following inscription :

In memory of
Admiral Sir Pulteney Malcolm, G.C.B.,
Born at Burnfoot of Esk, Dumfries-shire.
Died at East Lodge, Middlesex, on the 20th of July, 1838,
in his 70th year.
As an officer, distinguished in every rank, by his skill,
zeal and courage ;
Well tried in the battle and the breeze ;
And by a mild but efficient system of discipline.
Thrice appointed by his sovereign to the command-in-chief
of a British fleet;
on one occasion co-operating with a French squadron,
which he also had the honour of commanding.
Whilst he supported the honour of the British flag,
he obtained the respect and esteem, not only of our allies,
but of those against whom
hostilities were commenced or in contemplation,
which, by his conciliatory and moderate conduct,
he contributed to terminate or avert.
Active and amiable in all the duties and relations of
private life, whenever his services were not required at sea,
he passed most of his time in his native Eskdale,
where his kindness to all classes,
and his indefatigable endeavours to promote their welfare,
will be as fully appreciated as his public services have
been by other friends, not only of the United Service,
but of every rank and profession of civil life,
by whom this Monument has been erected.

Opposite is a monument to the Hon. M. Elphinstone, by M. Noble, with the following inscription :—

Honourable Mountstuart Elphinstone,
Member of the Indian Civil Service, Governor of Bombay,

and historian of early India.

Born MDCCLXXIX.   Died MDCCCLIX.

This monument was erected by public subscription, in admiration of his character, and in gratitude for his services. MDCCCLXIII.

In the recess under the window, is Lord Rodney's monument. The group represents History seated, and recording the achievements of the hero, as Fame narrates them, pointing to his statue while she speaks. On the pedestal is written:

Erected at the public expense to the memory of
GEORGE BRYDGES RODNEY, K.B.,
Lord Rodney, Vice-Admiral of England,
as a testimony of the gallant and important services
which he rendered to his country, in many memorable
engagements, and especially in that of 12th April, 1782,
when a brilliant and decisive victory was obtained
over the French fleet, and an
effectual protection was afforded to the West Indian
Islands, and to the commercial interests of this kingdom,
in the very crisis of the American War.
Lord Rodney was born in 1718,—died 24th of May, 1792.

Sir Thomas Picton's monument, by Gahagan, comes next. A group in front of the hero's bust, represents Genius leaning on the shoulder of Valour, receiving a wreath of laurel at the hands of Victory. On the pillar which supports the bust, are the insignia of several orders of Knighthood—the Bath, the Grand Cross, and the Portuguese Order of the Tower and Sword. The inscription is:

Erected at the public expense
to Lieutenant-General Sir THOMAS PICTON, K.G., C.B.,
who, after distinguishing himself in the victories of
Buzaco, Fuentes de Onor, Ciudad Rodrigo, Badajos,
Vittoria, the Pyrenees, Orthes, and Toulouse,
terminating his long and glorious military service,
in the ever-memorable battle of Waterloo,
to the splendid success of which
his genius and valour eminently contributed,
on the 18th of June, 1815.

Adjoining is a monument to General Napier, by Adams, the inscription is:

General WILLIAM FRANCIS PATRICK NAPIER,
Historian of the Peninsular War,
Born 1785.   Died 1860.

Opposite to this, against the great pier, stands a collossal statue of Lord St. Vincent, who is represented resting on his telescope. It is the work of Mr. Bailey. The bas-relief indicates History recording the hero's name on a pyramid, and Victory mourning his loss. Inscription:

Erected at the public expense, to the memory of
JOHN, EARL OF ST. VINCENT,
as a testimony of his distinguished eminence in the
naval service of his country,
and as a particular memorial of the glorious and important
victory which he gained over the Spanish fleet,
off Cape St. Vincent, on the 14th of February, 1797,
He died on the 13th of March, 1823.

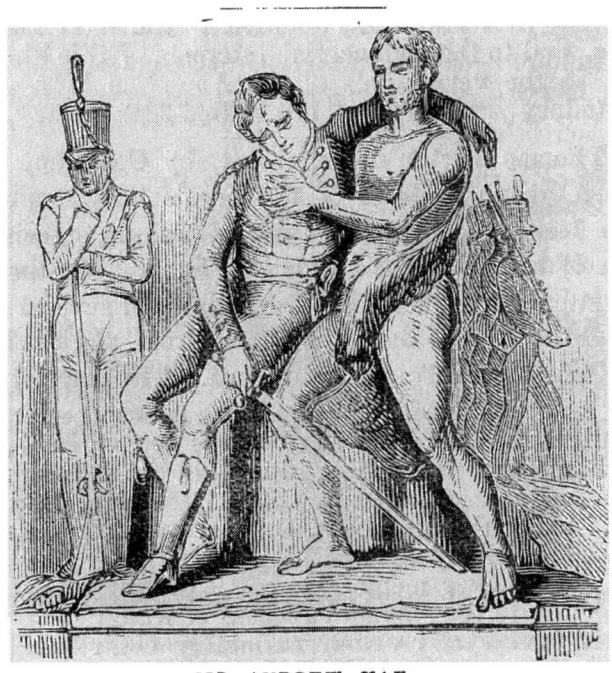

SIR ANDREW HAY.

Near the North door is the monument of Sir Andrew Hay. It is by Mr. H. Hopper, and depicts the brave officer in the arms of valour; a sentinel is seen in an attitude of grief, and in the back ground is the guard marching its rounds.

Erected at the public expense, to the memory of
Major-General ANDREW HAY,
He was born in the County of Banff, in Scotland,
and fell on the 14th of April, 1814,
before the fortress of Bayonne, in France,
in the 52nd year of his age, and the 34th of his services,
closing a military life marked by
zeal, prompt decision, and signal intrepidity.

Passing from the north door, towards the centre area, we find on the left hand, against the pier, the monument of Major-General Dundas, by Mr. Bacon, Junr. Britannia is attended by Sensibility; and the Genius of Britain is crowning the hero with laurel. On the pedestal, Britannia is seen defending Liberty against Fraud and Rebellion. The inscription is:

Major-General THOMAS DUNDAS,
died June 3rd, 1794, aged 44 years;
the best tribute to whose merit and public services
will be found in the following vote of the House of Commons
for the erection of this memorial.

June 5th, 1795. "Resolved, *nemine contradicente*, that an humble address be presented to his Majesty, that he will be graciously pleased to give directions that a monument be erected in the Cathedral Church of St. Paul, London, to the memory of Major-General Dundas, as a testimony of the grateful sense entertained by this House, of the eminent services which he rendered to his country, particularly in the reduction of the French West India Islands."

In the panel above, is a tabular monument to Generals Mackenzie and Langworth, executed by Manning. Victory s seen bewailing their loss, while two of Britain's sons re-

count their brave and valorous deeds. Two wreaths rest
against the tomb. The youths, one of whom has his helmet on, the other being decorated with a wreath of oak,
are well depicted; whilst the one is displaying to the other
the French Imperial Eagle, broken. The Inscription is:

National Monument
To Major-General J. R. MACKENZIE,
and Brigadier-General R. LANGWORTH,
who fell at Talavera, July 26th, 1809.

Against the opposite pier is Capt. Faulknor's monument
by Rossi. Neptune, seated on a rock, catches the falling
sailor, who, in the moment of death is crowned by Victory.
Underneath is written:

This Monument was erected by the British Parliament
to commemorate the gallant conduct
of Captain ROBERT FAULKNOR,
who on the 5th of Jan., 1795, in the 32nd year of his age,
and in the moment of victory,
was killed on board the *Blanche* Frigate, while engaging
La Pique, a French Frigate of very superior force.

The circumstances of determined bravery that distinguished this action, which lasted five hours, deserves to
be recorded. Captain Faulknor having observed the great
superiority of the enemy, and lost most of his mast and
rigging, watched an opportunity of the bowsprit of *La
Pique* coming athwart the *Blanche*, with his own hands
lashed it to the capstan, and thus converted the whole
stern of the *Blanche* into one Battery; but unfortunately,
soon after this bold and daring manœuvre, he was shot
through the heart.

In the panel above, is a monument to Generals Craufurd
and Makinnon, by Mr. Bacon, Junr. A highlander is
mourning over their tomb, while Victory crowns their
standard with a wreath. The British Lion is represented
with his paw upon the fallen Eagle; and a shield bearing
the arms of Spain, denotes the country where they
truggled with the French. There is inscribed:—

Erected by the Nation
to Major-General ROBERT CRAUFURD,
and Major-General HENRY MACKINNON,
who fell at Ciudad Rodrigo, January 18th, 1812.

We have now inspected all the monuments on the floor
of the Cathedral, but before descending into the Crypt, the
Choir and Organ demands our attention. The visitor that
knew the Choir formerly, when the Organ stood over the
entrance, will be agreeably surprised at the great alteration
and improved appearance, causing an uninterrupted view
from east to west, the enlarged altar, and many additional
seats covering that part of the floor of the Cathedral im_
mediately under the dome.

The Organ was originally built by that celebrated artist,
Bernard Schmidt, better known in England by the name
of Father Smith, about the year 1694; since that time,
some very important improvements have been made, and
quite recently it has been removed and divided. The present Organ, which contains nearly 60 sounding stops, and
4 manuals, is divided into three parts, the swell and choir
organ being on the South side, the solo and great on the
North side, and the pedal organ (which contains 2 stops
of 32 ft.) under one of the arches. The bellows, which
are very capacious, are placed in the crypt, near the East
end of the Cathedral, and are blown by three powerful
hydraulic machines; the air is thence brought to reservoirs
in various parts of the instrument by means of zinc tubing.
The connection between the differently situated portions
of the organ are by a new method, patented by Mr. Willis,
and although there is necessarily a great distance between
them, the touch answers instantaneously to the performer.
Many of Smith's magnificent stops are incorporated into
the pipe work. The splendid effect now produced is more
than equal to any instrument of the kind, especially in the

hands of such a talented musician as Dr. Stainer, the successor to Sir John Goss, who for many years held the post of organist.

Anciently, none but the clergy were admitted into the choir of a Cathedral, or chancel of a church; the laity remaining without, in the nave, during the whole service. It was considered a very great favour, as late as 1630, that the magistracy of London were admitted into the choir of St. Paul's, and females were not admitted until the last century. Choral service is held twice every week-day, at. ten in the morning, and at four in the afternoon; and three times on Sundays, at half-past ten in the morning, quarter-past three in the afternoon, and at seven in the evening; sermons being preached on Holy-days, and every Wednesday and Friday in Lent. The sermons on Sunday morning are preached by Clergymen selected by the Bishop of London, in the afternoon by the Residentiary Canons, each of whom takes a month in turn, and in the evening by various Clergymen selected by the Bishop, Dean, and Canons.

Along each side of the Choir is a range of fifteen stalls, with rows of seats in front of them, for the minor canons, lay vicars, and choristers. In the centre of the north range is the Lord Mayor's stall, adorned with the city sword and mace, and some other devices; opposite to it is the stall of the Bishop of the diocese, with the ancient episcopal emblem above it—a pelican feeding her young from her own breast. The Lectern, from which the lessons are read, formerly stood towards the east end of the choir, but is now removed and placed under the dome; it consists entirely of brass, richly gilt; the Bible rests upon an eagle with expanded wings. At the extremity of the South range of stalls, is the episcopal throne or chair of state, and decorated with richly sculptured flowers and fruit, surmounted by a mitre. The stalls in the choir are adorned with perhaps the finest carvings in the world; they were executed by Grinlin Gibbons, who was appointed Master Sculptor to George I. in 1712, and died in 1721.

The members of the Cathedral, consist of the Dean, four Canons Residentiary, 30 Prebendaries, 9 Minor Canons, and six Vicars Choral. There is a sermon preached annually, in May, on behalf of the Corporation of the Sons of the Clergy, when the Archbishops and Bishops, with the Lord Mayor, Aldermen, and Sheriffs, attend, and usually some member of the Royal Family; additional anthems are upon this occasion introduced in the service, and the choir increased in strength. The custom originated in 1655, when a sermon was preached by the Rev. G. Hall, to an assembly of the sons of such of the clergy, as with their families, had been reduced to indigence in consequence of the Parliamentary sequestrations in the time of the Commonwealth; King Charles II. afterwards granted a charter to the Society under the above title. These services were formerly made to combine a grand performance of sacred music, and no person was admitted except on condition of contributing gold as he entered; but this being thought unbecoming a sacred edifice, was abolished in 1843, and the public are admitted freely, the collection being made by plates held at the door, that such as are disposed may contribute as they leave the church.

Having inspected the choir, we are again in the body of the church, at which this is a fit time to glance. Before us is the central area—an octagon formed by eight massive piers, four of which are forty feet wide, and the others twenty-eight feet. In this area, beneath the dome, the charity children of the Parochial Schools of London, used to assemble on the first Thursday in June; this annual festival was first held in St. Paul's in 1782, and the sermon was preached by Dr. Porteous, Bishop of London.

The dome has an exceedingly light and elegant appearance; the cupola of the Pantheon at Rome is no higher within than its diameter; the dome of St. Peter's at Rome is as high as two diameters; the architect of St. Paul's has wisely adopted the mean—a diameter and a half. The whole vault of the cathedral consists of twenty-four cupolas cut off so as to be semi-circular, with segments to join to the great arches one way, these being cut across with eliptical cylinders the other way, to let in the upper light of the nave; but in the aisle the smaller cupolas are cut into semi-circular sections both ways. The nave is divided into three portions, a middle and two side aisles, by rows of pillars; a division considered essential to the character of a Cathedral, but which Wren is said to have felt to be so injurious to the general effect, that when compelled to introduce them, he shed tears of disappointment.

The visitor having completed the circuit of the floor of the Cathedral, should now descend into the Crypt, by the door near Howard's Monument.

The Crypt is divided, like the body of the Cathedral, into three parts by immense pillars, 40 feet square, and each of the side avenues is lighted by windows opening into the Church-yard; the north aisle was used as a burying place for the parishoners of St. Faith's. The eastern end is now used as a chapel, where service is held on week days at 8 a.m. & 8 p.m., and in which are preserved some fragments of the Old Cathedral, collected after the Great Fire, which consist of effigies of Sir Thomas Heneage, Chancellor of the Duchy of Lancaster, 1594; Anna, his wife, 1592; Sir Nicholas Bacon, father of the Lord Chancellor Bacon, 1597; Sir William Cockayne, 1626; Sir William Hewit, 1599; and Joannes Wolleius, latin secretary to Queen Elizabeth, 1595. The mosaic floor which has recently been laid down in this part is intended to be continued throughout the crypt. Near this spot has lately been erected a bust of the Rev. H. Venn, who died 13th of January, 1873, aged 77, a Prebendary of this Cathedral, and for 30 years honorary secretary of the Church Missionary Society. Also a tablet recently erected in memory of the late Miss Hackett.

In these vaults lie the remains of some of our most celebrated painters: Sir Joshua Reynolds, (died Feb. 23, 1792), James Barry, (Feb. 22, 1806), John Opie, (April 29, 1807), Benjamin West, (March 11, 1820), Sir Thomas Lawrence, (January 7, 1830), Henry Fuseli, (April 16, 1825). Robert Mylne, the Architect, who designed and constructed Blackfriars Bridge, (recently rebuilt), he died May 5, 1811; John Rennie, the Engineer, to whom we owe Waterloo and Southwark Bridges, he died Oct. 4th, 1821; Lord Chancellor Rosslyn, Dr. Boyce, the musical composer, Sir Edwin Landseer, R.A. (died Oct. 1, 1873), J. H. Foley, R.A. (died Aug. 27, 1874); and the following dignitaries of the Cathedral: Dean Milman, (died Sept. 24, 1868), Archdeacon Hale, (died Nov. 27th, 1870), Canon Melvill, (died Feb. 9, 1871). In the South aisle, towards the eastern end, and on the spot where the high altar of old stood, lie the remains of Sir Christopher Wren. A plain slab bears this inscription:

Here lieth
Sir CHRISTOPHER WREN, KNT.,
the Builder of this Cathedral Church of St. Paul,
who died in the year of our Lord, 1723,
and of his age, 91.

Near him lie the remains of his sister, Mrs. Holder; and of his only daughter, Jane, and one or two other relatives.

We now pass towards the enclosed portion of the crypt, here a plain slab marks the spot where Attwood, (many years organist of the Cathedral), is buried, also near, rest the remains of General Picton, whose monument we have already described; it may not be generally known, that Picton's remains were deposited in the burial ground of St. Martin's-in-the-Fields, and it was not until the year 1859 they were brought here. The visitor now descends two or three steps to the chamber which was specially prepared to receive the remains of the great Duke of Wellington; the Sarcophagus is of Cornwall Porphyry, in two pieces, the lower part contains the coffin, and is then covered by the upper part, or lid; it weighs some sixteen or seventeen tons. The inscription is thus :—

ARTHUR, DUKE OF WELLINGTON,
Born May 1st, 1769. Died September 14th, 1852.

The inner coffin, or pine shell, wherein the body is placed, was made by the Duke's own carpenter at Walmer. It is placed in a lead coffin, of twice the usual thickness and strength; and this, in a coffin of English oak, handsomely finished.

The outer coffin, or case, is of solid Spanish mahogany, covered with the richest crimson Genoa velvet. It is panelled with large gilt nails, and the ducal coronet engraved within the several gilt angle-plates; and at the sides and ends are large ring handles. In the lower portion of the upper panel of the lid are the Duke's arms; and in the centre of the foot panel is the Star of the Order of the Garter. The central or inscription plate is gilt, and bears the following:

"The Most High, Mighty, and Most Noble Prince Arthur, Duke and Marquis of Wellington, Marquis of Douro, Earl of Wellington, Viscount Wellington of Talavera and of Wellington, and Baron Douro of Wellesley, Knight of the Most Noble Order of the Garter, Knight Grand Cross of the Most Honourable Order of the Bath,

one of Her Majesty's Most Honourable Privy Council, and
Field Marshal and Commander-in-Chief of Her Majesty's
Forces. Born 1st May, 1769; Died 14th Sept. 1852."

The lead, oak and mahogany coffins were made by
Messrs. Dowbiggin and Holland, of Mount St., Grosvenor
Square; the outer coffin is altogether very handsome, but
not so sumptuous in its appointments as it would have
been, had it been expressly made for a State Funeral; the
wishes of Her Majesty not officially being known at the
time the order for the coffin was given to the undertakers.

We may here mention that on the day of the funeral
(Nov. 18th, 1852), the body was lowered through the centre of the floor, under the dome, and rested on the top of
Nelson's Tomb, for more than twelve months, when it was
again removed, but was not finally deposited in its present
resting place until April 1858, in the presence of the Dean
(Dr. Milman), the present Duke and others. The walls
are decorated with polished Aberdeen granite.

A few paces will bring us to the centre of the crypt,
where rests the remains of Nelson, Collingwood and
Northesk. The upper part of the Sarcophagus of Nelson,
is of Black Marble, surmounted with a coronet and cushion,
(it was originally intended to be used for the tomb of
Cardinal Wolsey), and bears this simple inscription:

HORATIO, VISCOUNT NELSON.

The remains of Lord Collingwood and Earl Northesk
are deposited on either side.

As the visitor proceeds, two tabular monuments demand
notice, one to Capt. Cook, and the other to Capt. Duff;
(both of whom were killed in the memorable battle of
Trafalgar), they have been recently placed here to allow
space for the reconstruction of the Organ, at the entrance
to the choir. Ascending two or three steps, we pass on
to the West end of the crypt, where is placed the Funeral

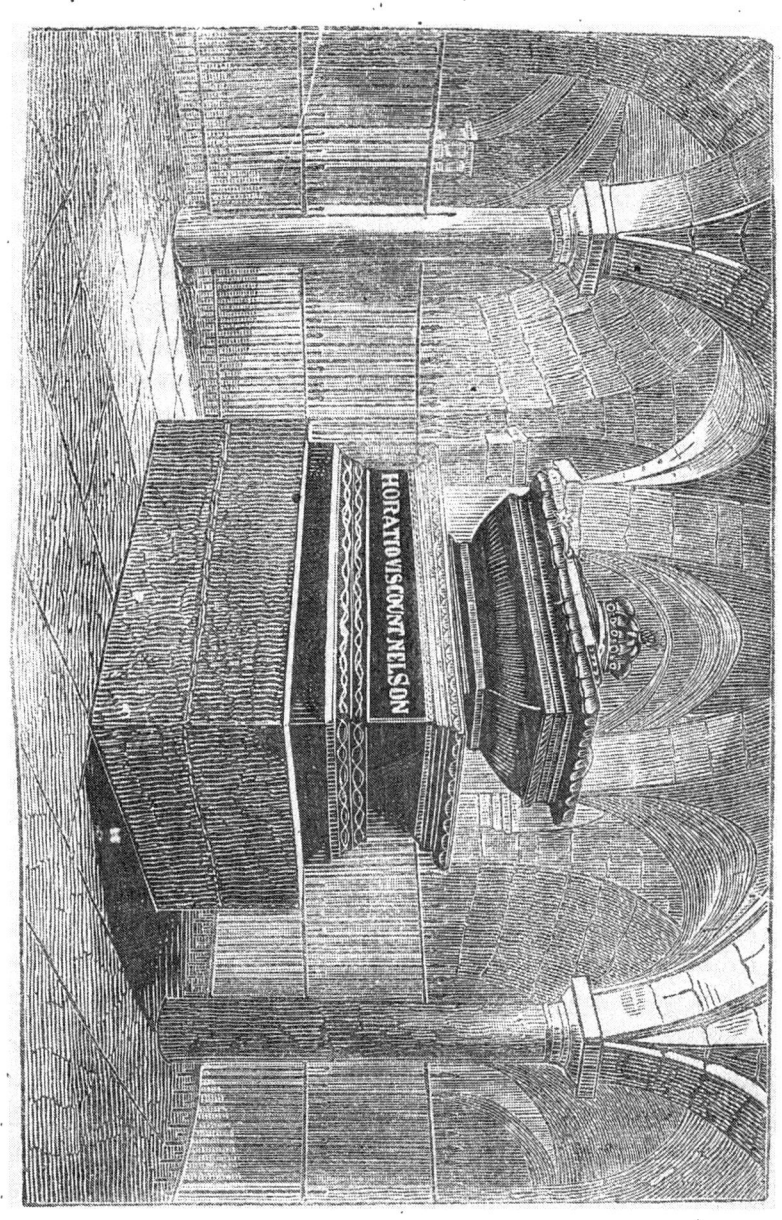

Car, on which the body of the Duke of Wellington was conveyed to the Cathedral, drawn by twelve black horses ; this massive piece of workmanship was cast from guns taken in the various actions which are enumerated on both sides; for a full description of the Funeral, &c., of this Great Hero, see Dean Milman's "Annals of St. Paul's."

The visitor now returns to the floor of the Cathedral, and proceeds (by the door in the South Transept), up the stairs, leading to the Whispering Gallery (by 260 easy steps), to the Upper Gallery (560 steps), and to the Ball (616 steps), whence there is a splendid view of the metropolis.

Arrived about half way up to the Whispering Gallery, we reach a door on the right, leading to the Library, the flooring of which consists of 2376 pieces of oak, skilfully inlaid without a single nail or peg. The Library contains about 9000 volumes, and a few ancient manuscripts, said to be the remains of the old monastic library, which was dispersed at the Reformation. Here is also a fine portrait of Dr. Compton, who was Bishop of London during the whole time the present Cathedral was building.

We next come to a flight of steps, called the Geometrical Stairs—the first ever made in England, which are so ingeniously constructed that all the ninety hang together without any visible support, resting on the bottom step. They seem to have been meant for a private way to the Library.

We now ascend to the Great Bell, which we find suspended 40 feet from the floor. It is 10 feet in diameter, the metal is 10 inches thick, and weighs 11,474 lbs. The tone is very fine, and is the musical note A, concert pitch. The hour is struck upon the Bell by a hammer, weighing 145lbs., which is drawn up by a wire in the clock-works, and then falls on the outside brim of the Bell by its own weight. The clapper, which weighs 180lbs., is only used to toll the Bell, on the death of any of the royal family, or of the Archbishop of Canterbury, the Bishop of London, the Dean of St. Paul's, or the Lord Mayor. The quarters are struck on two smaller bells underneath. The Great Bell was originally cast in the reign of Edward I., and hung at Westminster Hall gate, to notify the hour to the Judges; it was first called "Edward of Westminster," afterwards "Westminster Tom; William III. gave it to the present Cathedral, where it was brought on new year's day, 1699, but it has since been twice recast with additional metal ; it then weighed only 8,271 lbs.

The Clock next claims attention. It has two faces towards the streets, one looking to the west, the other to the south; each of them is 57 feet in circumference, or nearly 20 feet in diameter. The minute hand in each is 9 feet 8 inches long, and weighs 75 lbs.; the hour hand, 5 feet 9 inches long, and weighing 44 lbs. The hour figures are 2 feet 2½ inches long. The pendulum is 16 feet in length; the weight at the bottom is 108 lbs.; yet it is suspended by a spring no thicker than a shilling. It beats 30 times in a minute, or once in two seconds.

The Whispering Gallery is the next object of interest. It runs entirely round the base of the Cupola, and is 140 yards in circumference, having an elegant iron railing in front of it. It is so constructed, that the least whisper is heard on the opposite side, at a distance of 140 feet, as if it were a loud voice close to the ear. The shutting of the door, which resounds like the discharge of artillery, if allowed to fall by its own weight, is now discontinued, from a fear that the vibration would in time injure the building.

The paintings, in the eight compartments of the dome, are best seen from this gallery. They represent the leading events in the life of St. Paul, to whom the church is dedicated; his miraculous conversion on the way to Damascus—his striking Elymas, the sorcerer, blind—the proffered sacrifice at Lystra—the conversion of the jailor at Phillipi—his preaching on Mars Hill—the burning of the Magical books at Ephesus—his defence before Agrippa, and his shipwreck off Melita. It is said, that Sir James Thornhill, who painted this series, and was paid 40s. per square yard, retiring gradually a few steps to mark the effect of the finishing touches he had just given to the head of one of the apostles, had unconsciously reached the extremity of the scaffolding, and would by the next step have been precipitated to the floor below, when a by-stander observing that there was no time to explain his danger, snatched a brush full of paint and dashed it at the picture on the wall; Sir James, rushing forward to save his painting, saved his life.

The two large Mosaic Pictures in the spandrils of the dome, were executed by Salviati, one representing the prophet Isaiah, and the other, St. Matthew; it is intended to fill the remaining six with a similar work of art, the eight pictures to represent the four Evangelists, and the four major Prophets.

The next point of interest is the Stone Gallery, which surrounds the Dome; from this there is a fine view of London, spread out before the eye, the Bridges being especially striking. The towers of Churches rebuilt in consequence of the ravages of the great fire, will be noticed coated with black, like the dome of the Cathedral itself.

In passing now to the Upper or Golden Gallery, the visitor may mark that the architect has ingeniously introduced within the dome a brick cone, in order to raise the stone lantern which crowns the Cathedral, with its Ball and Cross; this lantern is reputed to weigh 700 tons. The outer dome is formed chiefly of wood, and covered with lead. A girdle of Portland stone encircles the lower part, in which is an enormous iron chain, weighing nearly five tons, inserted in a channel, cut for the purpose; the object being to render the crust more perpendicular than it could otherwise have been. Passing immediately under the outer dome, the stairs lead us to the Golden Gallery, surrounding the foot of the lantern; and here the visitor will pause to look on the great metropolis and the surrounding country, of which he has a magnificent view.

The Ball, to which we finally ascend, is six feet in diameter, and will hold 12 persons; its weight is 5,600 lbs. Thirty feet above it is the Cross, which weight 3,360 lbs. and is 15 feet high. A globe was a favourite emblem of the Roman emperors, upon which they used to plant the statue of victory; but since the time of Theodosius this latter has given place to the emblem of the Christian faith in symbolical decorations.

The Exterior of the Cathedral next demands some notice from us.

Approached from Ludgate Hill, the Western front has a very imposing aspect, towering proudly above the loftiest dwellings of London's thriving traders. In the front stands a marble statue of Queen Anne: on the base of which are figures representing Britannia with her spear, Gallia with her crown, Hibernia with her harp, America with her bow. This was the work of Francis Bird, who was paid £1,180 for it.

The Church is built of Portland stone. A handsome flight of steps of grey granite, conducts to the western or grand entrance, under a double portico of coupled columns, the lower being of the Corinthian, the upper of the Composite order; surmounted by a pediment, which is flanked on either side by a tower or steeple; one of these is the

belfry, in which has recently been placed a new peal of
twelve bells, and the other the Clock tower; in front of
them are statues representing the four evangelists, in a
recumbent posture. The entablature on the pediment
between these towers, contains a representation of the
Conversion of St. Paul, sculptured by Francis Bird, the
best British artist of his day; for which he received £650.
Over the pediment are three statues eleven feet high. St.
Paul is intended by the colossal figure on the apex, St.
Peter standing on his right hand, and St. James on his
left. It was the original intent of Wren, to have but a
single series of pillars in the portico, ascending nearly
90 feet from the ground; but it was found impossible to
procure from the Portland quarries blocks of sufficient
dimensions for this purpose.

There is an entrance also both in the north and south
transepts, each approached by a flight of steps of black
marble, and grey granite. These two porticos are semi-
circular, and consist each of a dome supported by six
Corinthian columns. The entablature upon the pediment
on the north side, presents a carving of the royal arms,
supported by angels. The south has a phœnix, (sculptured by Cibber, the father of the well-known actor),
with the word "Resurgam"—I shall rise again,—for
this his charge was £106. It is said that when Sir
Christopher Wren was marking out the ground to begin
the edifice, after the great fire, a man was desired to bring
a flat stone from one of the heaps of ruins, in order to in-
dicate where the centre of the dome should be; and when
the stone had been duly placed, it was found to present
on its surface in large letters the word RESURGAM; which
was regarded as a good omen, and worthy to be commemorated.

The apse, or eastern end of the Church is semi-circular,

and in a plain style of architecture. One of the few deco-rations is an imperial crown, with the letters " W.M." beneath it, encircled by palm branches; commemorating the completion of this part of the Cathedral during the reign of William and Mary.

The ground plan of the Cathedral is a latin cross, with an additional arm or transept at the west end, to give breadth to the grand front; there being also a semi-circular projection at the east end for the altar, the projections in the transepts for the north and south porticos. The dome rises from the intersection of the nave and transepts.

The entire length of the church, from east to west, is 500 feet; its breadth at the western entrance, 180 feet; at the transept, 250 feet; the general height of the wall, about 90 feet. The choir is 165 feet long. The entire circumference of the building is 2,292 feet. The height to the top of the cross is 352 feet from the floor of the church, or 360 feet from the pavement in the street. The western towers are 222 feet high. The exterior diameter of the dome is 189 feet.

The church covers 2 acres, 16 perches, and 70 feet. The cemetery, in the midst of which it stands, is enclosed by an iron balustrade, standing on a dwarf stone wall. The balustrades are 5 feet 6 inches in height.

The whole cost of the Cathedral, was £747,954 2s. 9d.

Paul's cross, at which sermons were formerly delivered in the open air, stood in the enclosure, on the north side of the church, a little eastward of the centre. It was taken down at the commencement of the civil war, in the time ot Charles I. There are some ancient benefactions for Paul's Cross sermons, but they are now preached in the cathedral.

Before closing this brief account of the great cathedral it may be well to mention that during the last few years the public have contributed largely towards decorating.

the church, and several stained glass windows have been given, the first, the great Western Window, given by Thos. Brown, Esq., of the firm of Longman's, booksellers, the subject being the Conversion of St. Paul; the second, given by the Drapers' Company, subject, the Crucifixion; the third, given by the Goldsmiths' Company, subject, the Agony in the Garden; the fourth, given by N. Rogers, Esq., subject, the Ascension; the three last mentioned are placed in the apse, or eastern end of the choir: and a Memorial Window to the late W. Cotton, Esq., at the eastern end of the South Aisle, subject, St. Stephen's Martyrdom; also, recently added, two other stained glass windows, over the North West and South West entrances, the first mentioned representing St. Paul, given by H. F. Vernon, Esq., the other, St. Peter, given by the Rev. Dr. Vivian.

Some notice of the history of the Cathedral will now complete our work.

It is probable, that there was an ancient Druidic temple on this spot, devoted to the worship of some idol god; for when Sir Christopher Wren examined the ground, he found the remains of ancient Britons, who had been here interred, with the stone coffins of distinguished Saxons, and funeral vases and other traces of Roman sculpture; whilst Stowe has recorded, that in digging the foundation of the Ladye Chapel, attached to the old Cathedral, about A.D. 1313, there were found many scalps of oxen or kine, "confirming greatly the opinion of those which have reported, that of old time there had been a temple of Jupiter, and that there was daily sacrifice of beasts." Be this as it may, the venerable Bede assures us that a christian church was erected here very soon after St. Augustine had commenced his work of converting England.

In 610, Ethelbert, king of Kent, undertook the building

of the church of St. Paul, and devoted certain manors and lands to its endowment. We also find Erkenwald, Bishop of London, who died about the year 686, devoting large sums of money towards the completion of the fabric. It is said to have been destroyed by fire in 961, and rebuilt within the following year. King Athelstan endowed it with " divers fair lordships "; and here king Ethelred was buried, and his son Edmond Ironside crowned. Canute, the Dane, who resided near St. Paul's, endowed its dean with some valuable land; and, according to Knighton, it was in the garden of his palace here, which extended to the river, that he rebuked his courtiers in their celebrated conversation by the rising tide.

William the Conqueror bestowed some large estates upon St. Paul's. Towards the close of his reign, in 1086, it was again destroyed by fire; and then, Maurice, Bishop of London, who had been also Chancellor, " conceived " (says Stowe), " the vast design of erecting the magnificent structure, which immediately preceded the present cathedral; a work that men at that time judged would never have been finished, it was so wonderful for length and breadth." The work, indeed, in those troublesome times, proceeded slowly; though some of the bishops devoted large sums to it, while much also was raised by the sale of Papal indulgences, and it was sufficiently advanced to allow the consecration in it of Anselm, Archbishop of Canterbury, in 1096, yet it was never finally completed until 1315, or 229 years from its commencement. The choir, however, had been consecrated in 1244, at which time the cross aisles were not commenced.

The old Cathedral thus completed, was built in the form of a cross, with north-and south aisles, a square tower being attached to each side of the west front; a square tower also rising from the point of intersection of the

transept with the nave and choir. The following is
Dugdale's account of its dimensions: .

	feet.
Length of the Church	690
Breadth	130
Height of West part	102
Height of the Choir	88
Height of the Body	150
Height of the Tower	260
Height of the Spire	520

Area of the limits, 3 acres and a half; of which, one rood
and a half and six perches were covered.

The great Clock was a splendid ornament; the figure ot
an angel pointed to the hour, in the sight of the passers by,
"a heavenly messenger marking the progress of time."

The Cathedral contained no less than seventy-six chantry
chapels; and there were sixty endowed anniversary obits,
or masses for the dead. It is supposed by Mr. Bradley,
that there must have been two hundred priests belonging
to it. In the nave stood a great cross, with a taper con-
stantly burning before it; and various statues of the Virgin
and Saints, in different parts, invited the oblations of the
worshipper.

As the Reformation dawned, the pomp and splendour of
the cathedral ceremonial began to diminish. On the 18th
of Sept. 1547, the Litany was first chanted at St. Paul's,
and the Epistle and Gospel read at High Mass, in the
English language. Two months afterwards, the rood and
the images of the saints were taken down. On February
2, 1548, the bearing of candles in the church was discontinued. On April 8, 1549 mass was put down. The high
altar was taken down, June 11, 1550. Nov. 1, 1552, the
new book of Common Prayer was first used; Bishop Rid-
ley preaching at the Cathedral on the occasion.

In February, 1445, the steeple of St. Paul's was fired by lightning; the injury was repaired, but with some delay. In June, 1561, it was again set on fire through the negligence of a workman, and was never rebuilt. The body of the church which had greatly suffered on this occasion, was speedily roofed in again; but the damage not being completely repaired, the fabric began to decay. In the reign of Charles I., Laud being Bishop of London, there was no less than £104,330 collected to put it into repair; but before the works were completed, the civil war broke out, and parliament seized both the money and materials. The whole of the church, except the choir, was then used for stables and shops for the accomodation of the soldiers, who also amused themselves in it by playing at nine pins, and other games.

At the restoration, a public subscription was collected under the auspices of Charles II. for repairing the edifice, but before the works were begun, the great fire broke out on the night of Sept. 2, 1666, and this noble building was a mass of smouldering ruins.

Sir Christopher Wren was the person fixed on to rebuild the Cathedral; and in December, 1672, his designs were finally approved by King Charles II. Above £126,000 were collected from the public in general, for this great national work; a duty on coals produced £5000 a year, and his Majesty contributed £1,000 a year. Wren was to have only £200 a year for superintending the works. Having removed 47,000 loads of rubbish, (the old walls being demolished with the battering ram), the first stone of the present Cathedral was laid, at the north east corner of the choir, June 21, 1675. The choir was opened for divine service, on the day of the Thanksgiving for the peace of Ryswick, December 2, 1697. The last or highest stone of the building was laid at the top of the lantern, in

1710; the whole structure being thus completed in thirty-five years, by one architect, Sir Christopher Wren; and by one master mason, Mr. T. Strong; under one prelate, Dr. Compton, Bishop of London. Shortly afterwards Queen Anne, with both houses of Parliament, attended Divine Service in the new Cathedral.

In 1773, Sir Joshua Reynolds, as president of the Royal Academy, made an offer, on the part of himself and some other artists, to supply gratuitously, a series of scriptural paintings, to relieve the heavy appearance of the large bare walls and piers; but the proposal was opposed by Archbishop Cornwallis, and the Bishop, Dr. Terrick, and was therefore abandoned. The church remained undecorated for several years more; the first monument admitted being that of Howard, the philanthropist, which was thrown open to public inspection, Feb. 23, 1796.

MEASUREMENT OF THE HEIGHT OF ST. PAUL'S.

	ft.	in.
From the Vaults to First Floor	20	0
From First Floor to Second Gallery	215	6
From Second Gallery to Third ditto	50	0
From Third Gallery to Golden ditto	6	1
From Floor of Church to top of Cross	352	9
Pavement outside to top of Cross	363	4

Milton Keynes UK
Ingram Content Group UK Ltd.
UKHW022250080124
435706UK00005B/283